let us play I SPY things that go!

kids play books by
© Miss Little Green

ready to match the correct letter with the right vehicle?

letters are not in alphabetical order, just like real i spy game.

i spy with my little
eye, something beginning with...

S is for...
Submarine!

i spy with my little
eye, something beginning with...

d is for...
Dump truck!

i spy with my little
eye, something beginning with...

b is for...

bus!

i spy with my little
eye, something beginning with...

t is for...
tractor!

i spy with my little
eye, something beginning with...

h is for...

helicopter!

i spy with my little
eye, something beginning with...

V is for...
van!

i spy with my little eye, something beginning with...

f is for... Fire truck!

i spy with my little
eye, something beginning with...

P is for...
Police car!

i spy with my little
eye, something beginning with...

C is for...

car!

i spy with my little
eye, something beginning with...

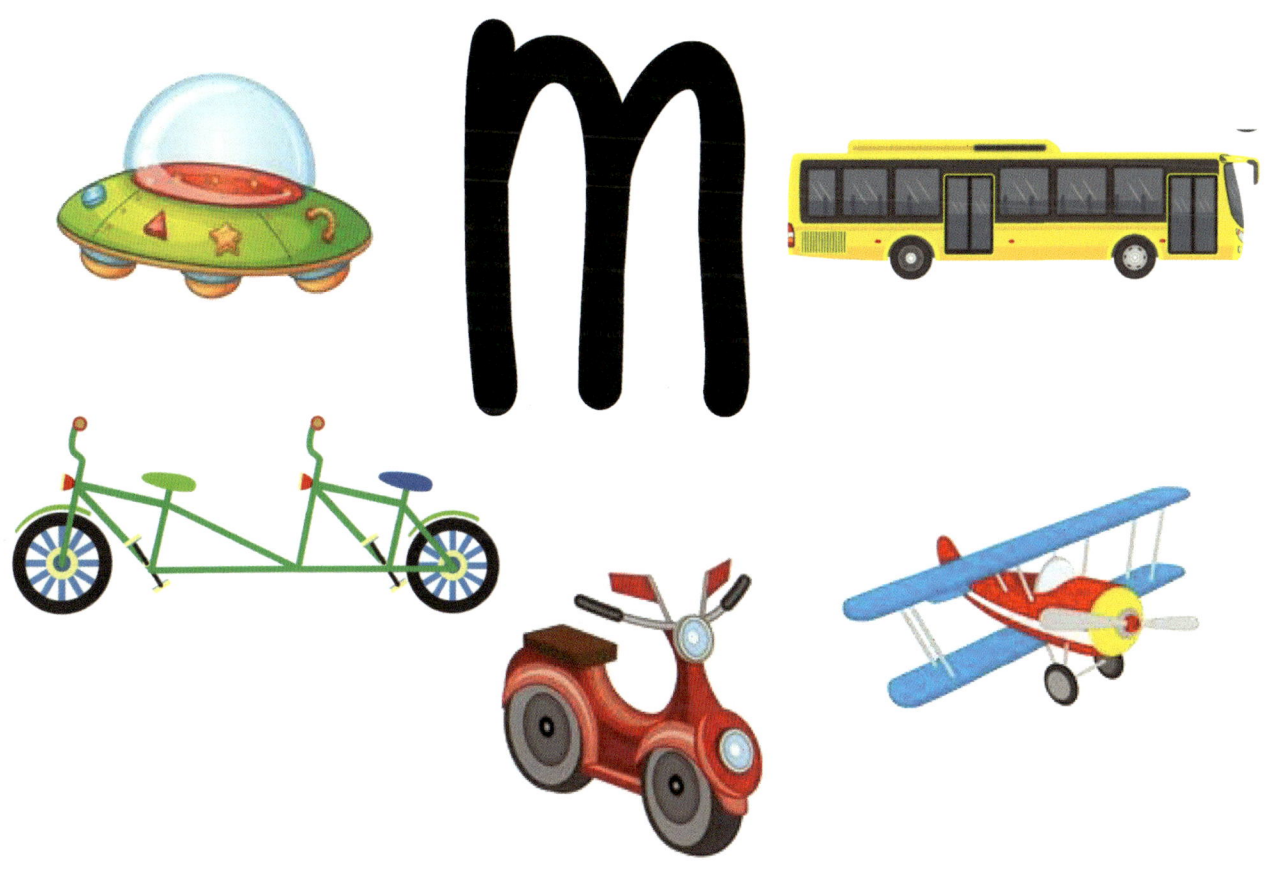

M is for...
motorcycle!

i spy with my little eye, something beginning with...

a is for... aeroplane!

i spy with my little
eye, something beginning with...

Y is for...
Yacht!

i spy with my little
eye, something beginning with...

b is for...
bicycle!

i spy with my little eye, something beginning with...

l is for... lorry!

i spy with my little
eye, something beginning with...

r is for...
rocket!

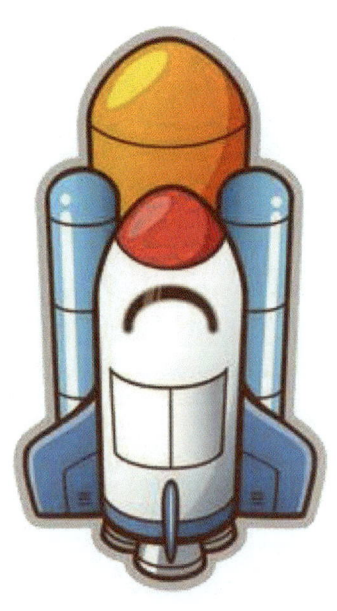

i spy with my little eye, something beginning with...

e is for...
Excavator!

i spy with my little
eye, something beginning with...

U is for... unicycle!

i spy with my little eye, something beginning with...

K is for...
kayak!

i spy with my little
eye, something beginning with...

i is for...
ice cream truck!

Printed in Great Britain
by Amazon